THE LATER YEARS OF BRITISH RAILWAYS 1980–1995

Volume One – The North of England and Scotland

Patrick Bennett

AMBERLEY

Author's Note

Railways do not easily lend themselves to precisely defined geographical areas, being essentially linear, and thus readers may find that my chapter headings are approximations of area rather than precisely defined. For example, areas of North Derbyshire and North Cheshire are included in this volume, although it could be argued that they are not part of Northern England. Similarly the line from Hull to Scarborough passes from the East Riding to North Yorkshire, but it seemed sensible to treat this as a single entity rather than deal with it in two separate chapters. Scotland was dealt with on a line-by-line basis, except for the chapter entitled 'Glasgow and South Western'.

The author and publisher would like to thank the following people for permission to use copyright material in this book: Ben Brooksbank for the photographs taken at Manchester Victoria, Stockport, Royston and Notton, and Sheffield; Geoffrey Skelsey for the photograph taken at Guide Bridge; Peter Groom for the photograph taken at Wigton.

First published 2017

Amberley Publishing
The Hill, Stroud
Gloucestershire, GL5 4EP

www.amberley-books.com

ISBN 978 1 4456 7432 2 (print)
ISBN 978 1 4456 7433 9 (ebook)

British Library Cataloguing in Publication Data.
A catalogue record for this book is available from the British Library.

Origination by Amberley Publishing.
Printed in the UK.

Contents

Introduction

The railway in 1980 had little changed since the 1960s. Certainly there were no more steam locomotives, but passenger trains consisted largely of carriages hauled by locomotives; many of these carriages were still steam-heated. The locomotives themselves were mostly constructed in the 1950s or early 1960s. Secondary services were provided by various types of multiple units from the same era. Freight traffic was still buoyant and marshalling yards busy. Much of the freight was still carried in short wheelbase wagons and there were numerous freight branches and sidings. Traditional signalling was still very much in evidence throughout the system, even on some main lines; except on the Southern, major electrification work had not progressed beyond the West Coast Main Line.

In 1980 BR was still one railway, the evidence for which was that everything was painted one colour! All this was about to change. In the 1980s, a whole series of multiple units was introduced, not just replacing the older types on similar duties, but also usurping loco-hauled trains on many routes; the Trans-Pennine service is a good example. In 1976 the High Speed Train had been introduced, and progressively replaced loco-hauled trains on the GWR and GNR routes. Many of the first generation locomotives and multiple units were withdrawn. Electrification was extended to the East Coast Main Line, the southern part of the Midland main line, and in East Anglia. Many of these changes were for the better but unfortunately many more were for the worse; the worst of the worst being sectorisation, an accountant's dream. Many freight traffics were lost, among these newspapers and parcels. Finally, in 1995 came privatisation – the explosion of the railway into a hundred fragments.

The photographs that appear in the following pages are very much a personal collection, reflecting my own interests and to some extent my own travels. During the course of the period this volume covers my methodology in taking photographs changed. In 1988 I realised that the railway was changing at an ever increasing rate with many of its features disappearing; so it was, that from that time onwards, I tended to concentrate my efforts on what was shortly to be lost forever. This included older types of locomotives and rolling stock, traditional signalling, and particularly freight flows, sidings and freight-only lines. I have also included, with their permission, a few photographs of the steam age, taken by Peter Groom and Ben Brooksbank, which I hope give a broader historical context. I am most grateful to them.

When compiling this book, twenty-two years after the last photograph was taken, what struck me very forcibly is that in this latter period the railway has changed to an even greater extent than in the preceding fifteen years. The passenger railway is now almost entirely in the hands of multiple units of various kinds. Freight has declined catastrophically, not least because of the closing down of the British mining industry. Many freight-only lines have closed, and whole swathes of freight infrastructure – sidings, terminals, marshalling yards – have been swept way. Traditional signalling is becoming an endangered species, with vast areas controlled by single centres. Electrification has proceeded apace, if not without problems, and there have been a number of stations reopened for passenger use. The result of all this change is that the vast majority of images in this book depict scenes that have gone forever. They are, in that sense, historic.

Putting together a work such as this, involving making a choice of hundreds of photographs from several thousand, will inevitably reflect the particular interests of the author. Nevertheless, I have tried to include as broad a sweep as possible of the railway that existed in the later years of BR and hope others will enjoy reading this book as much as I have enjoyed writing it.

Millay, France
April 2017

North of Manchester

This photograph gives a good impression of the steep bank up from Manchester Victoria, which came into use in January 1844. Gradients are as steep as 1 in 30 and 1 in 47 and initially the line was worked using stationary engines and ropes. No. 158906 in West Yorkshire PTE livery passes Miles Platting Junction with a service for Leeds. Miles Platting box was closed at the time of the North Manchester resignalling in 1998. 13 April 1991.

Another signal box that closed at the same time was Brewery Sidings, seen in the background. The line on the left is the Down West Goods (now abolished); the signals to the right control the lines coming from the Ashton branch, while the Class 150 is heading straight on to Manchester Victoria. 28 June 1991.

This was once an important junction. The line to the right led to Oldham, and on the left there was a branch to Middleton. This branch closed in 1964 and Middleton Junction station followed in 1966. The line to Oldham closed in 1963 but the track as far as Chadderton was retained to service the goods and coal depot at that location. At the time this photograph was taken (27 November 1988) the Chadderton line was still active but closed soon after. The signal box, which dates from 1882, was abolished in 1990. Nothing remains at this site. No. 155347 forms the 11.10 Leeds to Manchester Victoria.

A Class 142 'Pacer' in Greater Manchester PTE livery heads south past Castleton Junction. Castleton station, originally known by the unusual name of Blue Pits, can be glimpsed through the bridge. 7 September 1991.

Godley Junction was opened in 1886. It was the meeting point of the GC line from Manchester and the CLC branch from Woodley. It was renamed Godley in 1974 and renamed once more in 1986, this time becoming Godley East, following the opening of a new Godley station further west. A token service of one train a week continued until the station closed definitively in May 1995. On 22 January 1992, a Class 304 passes through without stopping.

Ashton Moss North Junction with the diverted 07.33 Edinburgh–Birmingham. This diversion was caused by engineering work at Manchester Piccadilly. The train is taking the line to Denton Junction and Stockport. The lines straight on lead to Ashton and Stalybridge. Of interest is the gantry on the left, a surviving remnant of the 1500 V dc electrification.

Above and right: East of Ashton Moss N. is Oldham, Ashton & Guide Bridge Junction signal box, which controlled the junction leading to Ashton Moss South. The signal box and junction have been abolished. The OAGBJ railway was a joint line owned by the GC and LNWR (yellow on the map). Only the southern section from Ashton Moss N. to Guide Bridge survives. 27 January 1992.

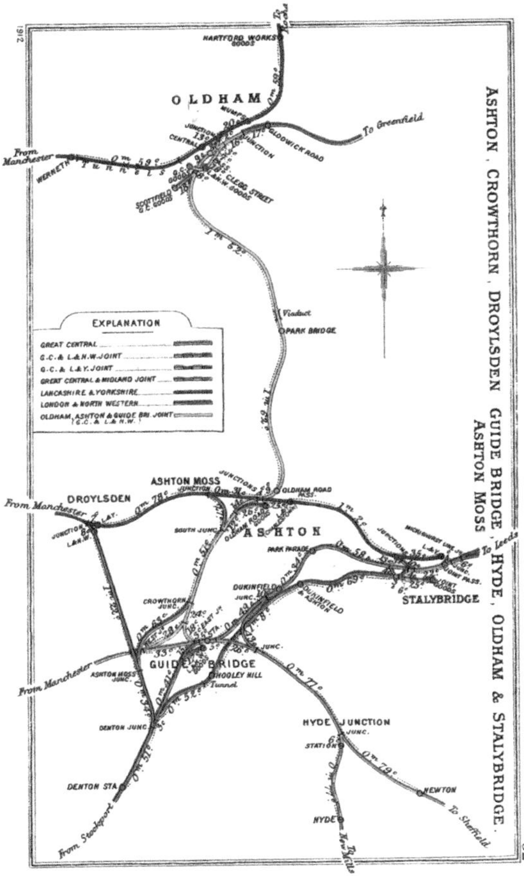

Manchester Victoria. On 25 October 1981 No. 25050 is the station pilot.

On 22 August 1964, a Stanier Class 5 4-6-0 heads through the station with an eastbound express. Meanwhile, Ivatt 2-6-0 No. 46452 and a 4F 0-6-0 wait for their turn on banking duties. (Photo: Ben Brooksbank)

The line from Manchester Victoria to Bury opened in 1879. It was not the first line to Bury but is the only one which survives. In 1916 the line was electrified using a unique 1,200 V dc third rail side contact system. This continued in use until the line was converted to a Metrolink line, the preparations for which can be seen in this photograph taken in April 1991, shortly before conversion to tram operation. The Class 504 units seen here passing Queen's Road signal box were introduced in 1959.

This scene is considerably changed as the Liverpool–Manchester line is now electrified. Eccles signal box has survived, due to the need to operate the points leading to the Weaste oil terminal line – the line seen on the left, which passes under the main line and runs alongside the Manchester Ship Canal. On 10 January 1994, No. 60007 hauls a rake of tanks towards the main line.

Guide Bridge

Guide Bridge station came into being with the opening of the Sheffield, Ashton-under-Lyne & Manchester Railway's Manchester–Sheffield line, which at that time was open only as far as Godley Toll Bar. Originally named Ashton and Hooley Hill, it became plain Ashton in February 1842, and Guide Bridge in July 1845. It became a junction with the opening of the SA&M line to Stalybridge, and the Manchester and Birmingham line from Stockport, both in the mid-1840s. The picture was completed with the opening of the OAGBJ line in 1861.

By the early 1980s there was just one diesel locomotive on BR left in original green livery – No. 40106. Following its entry into works for overhaul and repaint, there was much surprise to see it re-emerging back in green, as seen here at Guide Bridge in 1982, heading towards Manchester with a long parcels train.

Towards the end of their career the Class 40s became concentrated in the North West and were a common sight around Manchester. On the same afternoon another Class 40 heads past with a long rake of coal wagons.

Double-headed Class 40 workings were unusual, as we see another long train heading west on the same date. Two other Class 40s await their duties and on the extreme right are parked some of the redundant Class 76 locos.

Hard to believe that this is the same location. The mass of lines on the right have all been removed, leaving just the former slow lines. As well as removing the slow lines, the platforms and range of station buildings have all been demolished. 9 November 2016.

This photograph, taken in 1967, shows a Class 506 EMU and a Class 76-headed train on the fast lines at Guide Bridge. Everything seen here no longer exists, following rationalisation in the mid-1980s. (Photo: Geoffrey Skelsey)

South of Manchester

The railway reached Stockport from Manchester in July 1840. At that time the station was at the north end of the viaduct that spans the town. Stockport Edgeley wasn't opened until 1843. The original station was renamed Heaton Norris. It closed in 1959.

The Class 104 units were particularly associated with the Manchester to Buxton line. 6 May 1989 was the last day of operation for these units. A specially prepared unit comes off the viaduct as it enters Stockport station. The two-digit headcode box is made of cardboard!

Somewhat earlier, Fowler 2-6-4T No. 42363 stands at Stockport with the 10.20 Buxton–Manchester. This photograph was taken just two years before the Class 104s were introduced. (Photo: Ben Brooksbank, 26 March 1955)

A type of train sadly no longer with us is this Bolton–St Pancras parcels train, entering Stockport station headed by No. 47543. 26 June 1991.

Attracting attention from loco spotters is this unusual visitor to Stockport. Notice the Tinsley logo and shedplate, and also the unofficial name of *Nimrod*. No. 45052 was withdrawn in June 1988. The signal box is Stockport No. 1; under threat of closure for some time, but still in use at the time of writing (2017).

The Manchester, South Junction & Atrincham Railway was opened in 1849 and jointly managed by the Manchester & Birmingham and the Sheffield, Ashton & Manchester Railways (later LNW and GC). From the outset it was a busy commuter route and in 1931 it was electrified at 1500 V dc. In 1971 it was converted to 25 kV ac, to conform with the majority of the rest of the Manchester area. In 1991/2 it was converted to become part of the Metrolink tram network. In its last year of operation as a conventional railway, a Class 304 unit heads past Navigation Road signal box with a northbound service. The Saxby & Farmer box, dating from 1882, was closed that same year.

The line from Macclesfield to Marple Wharf Junction was opened by the Macclesfield, Bollington & Marple Railway in 1869. It was taken over by the MSL and North Staffs in 1871 and managed as a joint line. It was closed in 1970, apart from the short stub from Marple Wharf to Rose Hill. In 1988, green-liveried Class 108 set LO298 waits to leave Rose Hill with a service for Manchester Piccadilly.

In the early 1980s the Class 124 Trans-Pennine units were replaced by Class 31 loco-hauled trains. In 1986 the Hazel Grove chord was opened. This single line joined the Midland Railway New Mills South Junction to Cheadle line, with the LNW Manchester to Buxton line, thus enabling Trans–Pennine trains to call at the important station of Stockport and also continue to Liverpool without crossing the station throat at Manchester Piccadilly. On 5 April 1988, No. 31452 is seen on the chord heading towards Stockport, in charge of the 16.22 Sheffield–Liverpool.

At New Mills South Junction No. 31221 is seen with the 13.45 Liverpool–Sheffield. 6 April 1988.

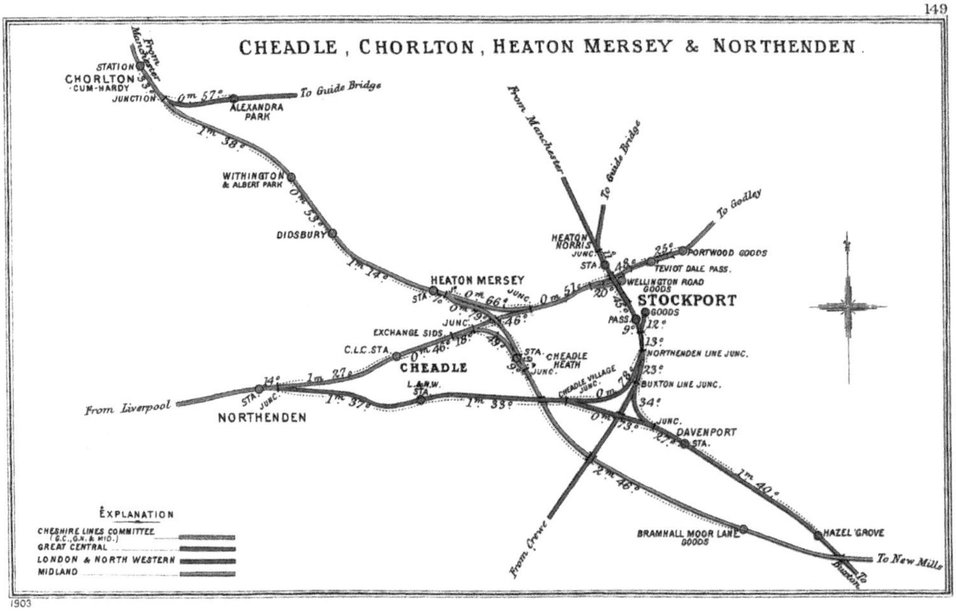

The Cheshire Lines Committee was formed by the MSL and GNR in 1865, joined a year later by the Midland Railway. The line from Woodley to Portwood (Stockport) was opened in 1863 and from Portwood to Broadheath via Skelton Junction in 1866. Broadheath to Cressington and London Road to Glazebrook opened in 1873.

At the site of Northenden station No. 37680 shunts a train of cement at the Blue Circle depot. The train originated at Earles Sidings in the Hope Valley. Northenden Junction signal box can just be seen beyond the bridge. 11 May 1993.

Skelton Junction was a three way junction, with lines to Warrington, Glazebrook and Altrincham. The train is a Manchester–Chester working. Passenger trains started using this line again when the Altrincham line became part of Metrolink. Skelton Junction signal box has since been demolished. 9 April 1991.

The Glazebrook line remained open as far as Partington for freight traffic. This is No. 47234 approaching Sinderland level crossing with a rake of LPG tanks. The Partington branch remains in place but traffic ceased shortly after this photograph was taken. 3 May 1993.

GLAZEBROOK & PARTINGTON

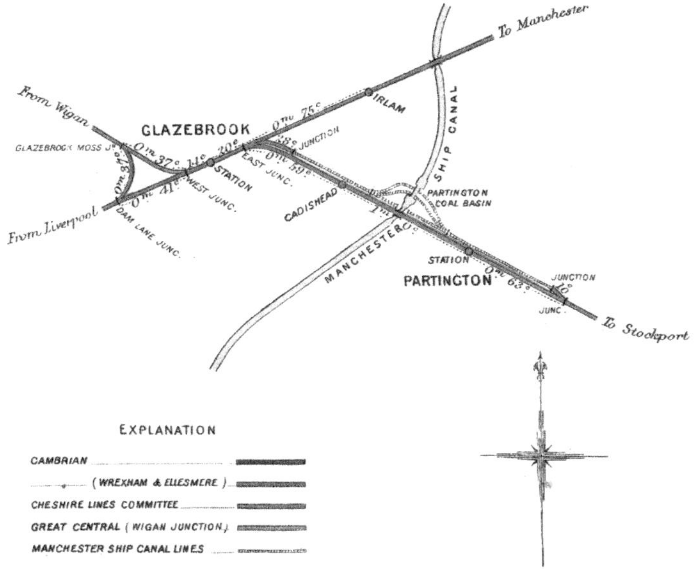

Glazebrook was at the other end of the Partington line, where it met the CLC Manchester–Liverpool route. At Cadishead were the works of British Tar Products. This traffic has ceased and the branch has been lifted.

On the Glazebrook branch is No. 56046 with train 6M67, empty tanks bound for Lindsey. 31 May 1995.

Merseyside and South Lancashire

In 1854 the Warrington & Stockport Railway opened the line from Broadheath to Warrington. The sections of lines between Garston and Widnes, and between Widnes and Warrington had previously been opened by the St Helens Canal & Railway Company. The line enjoyed a passenger service between Manchester and Liverpool until 1962, at which time it was withdrawn between Broadheath and Ditton junction.

The original line to Widnes station (originally called Runcorn Gap) was the one that can be seen going straight on in the background. This line led to a flat crossing with the line to St Helens. In order to avoid this, a new line (the Widnes Deviation) was built from Carterhouse Junction to West Deviation Junction. On this line a new station was built, which eventually became Widnes South. On 27 April 1995, No. 31142 is seen with a Ditton Junction–Warrington working. The men standing by the level crossing are waiting to take their cows across to the pasture on the left of the line, where they will stay until the autumn. The Carterhouse Junction box was abolished in 2006 and demolished the following year.

Above and below: In 1985 the line between Broadheath and Warrington was closed to all traffic. A short section as far as Latchford Junction was retained to allow trains from Walton Old Junction Yard to reach Fiddlers Ferry power station; this was accomplished by means of a reversal on this short section of line, as illustrated by these two photographs. No. 31174 hauls a train from the yard towards Latchford Sidings. Nos 20141 and 20013 now haul the train away from Latchford towards Fiddlers Ferry. The signal box is Arpley Junction. 24 June 1991.

No. 56029 approaches the site of Widnes South station with the Widnes Blue Circle–Earles Sidings cement empties. The Blue Circle cement depot at Widnes has since been closed down. The cooling towers of Fiddlers Ferry power station are seen in the background. 05 July 1994.

The Liverpool, Crosby & Southport Railway opened in 1848, being taken over by the Lancashire & Yorkshire in 1855. The line was electrified using the third rail system in 1904. In 1989 there were still thirteen signal and gate boxes between Bootle Junction and Southport; now there are none and the whole line is controlled from the Merseyrail Signalling Centre at Sandhills. In this photograph we see a pair of Class 508 units arriving at Birkdale with a service for Southport, one in Merseyrail livery. These units are due to be replaced in 2020 by units built by Stadler. 07 June 1992.

Above: LMS Class AM3 unit restored to its former glory stands at Southport. This unit, built in 1938, now resides in the Electric Railway Museum at Coventry. 17 September 1989.

Right: A collection of signs at the level crossing at Duke Street. 23 October 1989.

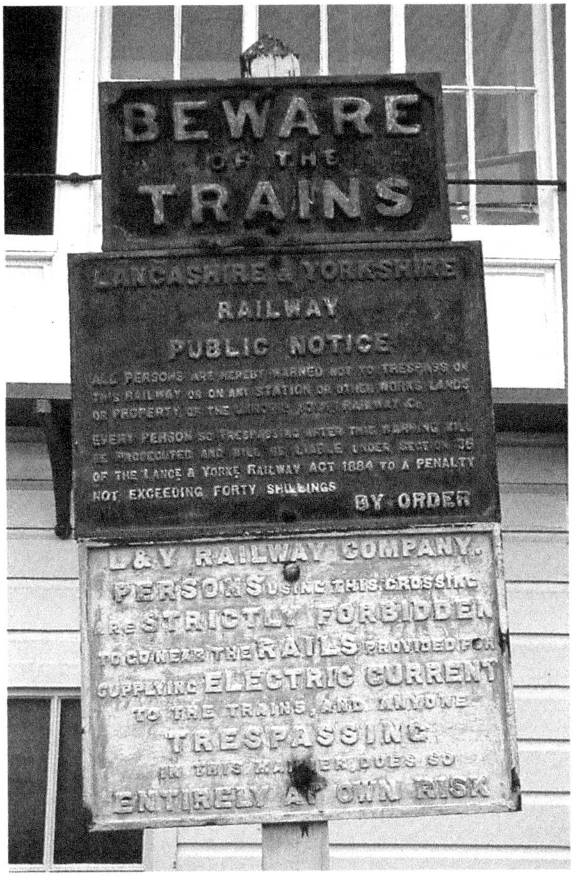

The East Lancashire Railway completed its line from Liverpool to Preston in 1848. In the early years of the twentieth century, the LYR progressively electrified the line, reaching Ormskirk in 1913.

A Class 507 unit approaches Town Green station with the 09.47 Liverpool Central to Ormskirk. The signal box was an LMS Type 13 (ARP) box built 1949. It was abolished in 1994 when the line was resignalled. Yet another line controlled from the Merseyrail Centre. 20 June 1992.

A former Class 501 unit, converted for Sandite duties, passes through Maghull Station. The Class 501 units were built in 1955/56 and all were withdrawn by 1985. The last Sandite unit was withdrawn in 2002. 1 October 1989.

In May 1992 a Class 142 'Pacer' arrives at Huyton with a service for Liverpool. This scene has changed totally. There are now four electrified lines and the semaphore signals together with the signal box have gone. 21 May 1992.

The Liverpool–Manchester railway was opened in 1830 but it was to be another forty-one years before the line from Huyton Junction to St Helens was constructed. This line has also been electrified and resignalled. Prescot signal box has been abolished and the line on the extreme left, which once led to the BICC factory, has been lifted. A Class 142 approaches Prescot station with the 15.25 Blackpool North to Liverpool Lime St. 21 May 1992.

St Helens, another location transformed by electrification and resignalling. No. 142023 is seen arriving with the 11.12 Wigan to Liverpool. The lines curving to the left at the far end of the platform lead to Hays Chemicals. 26 August 1994.

A Class 150 passes through St Helens Yard with the 11.37 Liverpool–Wigan North Western. The sidings have all been removed and the signal box has been abolished. 26 August 1994.

At Rainford Junction the driver of the 09.05 Wigan to Kirkby accepts the token for the following 5.25-mile single track section. 20 June 1992.

Heading south at Winwick Junction are Nos 47206 and 92030 with a test train. No. 92030 had worked the train over Shap, and the pair are heading back to Crewe. 2 May 1995.

No. 31444 heads south with a mail train, just south of Lostock Junction, the signal gantry of which can be seen in the background. The signal box was abolished shortly after this photograph was taken. Note that the third and fifth coaches are TPOs, which once had pick up/drop off equipment fitted. 20 May 1989.

No. 31465, in Regional Railways livery, heads the 17.33 Manchester Picadilly–Blackpool 'Club' train just north of Lostock Junction. 3 May 1995.

North Lancashire and Cumbria

The first railway to arrive in Preston was the Northern Union Railway from Wigan. This was followed in 1840 by three further railways: the Preston & Longridge; the Lancaster & Preston Junction, and the Bolton & Preston. Two more followed in 1846: the Liverpool, Ormskirk & Preston and the Blackburn & Preston.

The Grand Caledonian Junction Railway was a line envisaged by George Stephenson, which would have run from Lancaster to Carlisle along the Cumbrian coast. It never happened and the line that was built was as the result of a number of different companies' efforts over a number of years. In 1845 the Maryport & Carlisle Railway opened, followed by the Whitehaven Junction Railway, which linked Maryport with Whitehaven. The Furness Railway opened its line between Foxfield and Barrow-in-Furness, which was later extended to Ulverston. The Whitehaven & Furness Junction Railway was completed in 1855 and finally in 1857 the line became a through route with the opening of the Ulverston & Carnforth Railway.

The Preston & Wyre Harbour Company (P&W) opened its line to Fleetwood in July 1840. At that time Blackpool was an insignificant place and had to wait until April 1846 to be served by a branch from the main line. The line to Blackpool South had a protracted genesis. The P&W first opened a line from a junction, near Kirkham Junction, to Lytham. The Blackpool & Lytham Railway constructed a line from Lytham to Blackpool in 1863. However there was no connection between these two lines at Lytham. This did not come until 1874, after the absorption of all the Wyre peninsular lines jointly by the LYR and LNWR. In 1903 a further line, 'The New Line', was constructed between Kirkham and Blackpool South, taking a direct route. This line closed in 1965.

A photograph strangely evocative of rail travel thirty-six years ago, as a Class 108 unit simmers gently at Preston, waiting to depart with the 13.05 Preston–Colne. 25 October 1981.

At Preston, No. 40087 takes over a Leighton Buzzard–Blackpool Merrymaker excursion. 25 October 1981.

A Class 104 unit arrives at Bamber Bridge with the 10.35 Colne–Blackpool. Notice that the second vehicle has a white stripe along the body – this is an indication that this is one of the vehicles fitted with a modified type of suspension. 25 October 1981.

Kirkham and Wesham Junction on a busy Saturday afternoon in 1983 as trains return from Blackpool. A pair of Class 108 units on the slow line, headed for Leeds.

This pair of Class 120 units are somewhat unusual visitors to the area. They are en route to Manchester Victoria.

This Class 25 seems little troubled by its ten coach load. Considering the modest size of their engines, these locomotives were remarkably robust workhorses.

The London train, consisting of Mark 2 coaches, being taken as far as Preston by this Class 47. Kirkham and Wesham is the junction for the lines to Blackpool North and Blackpool South. The line to the left is to Blackpool South. Blackpool North is straight on. The line from Preston to Blackpool is due to be electrified by 2018, at which time the layout and signalling here will be considerably modified.

The magnificent array of signals seen in these two photographs will soon be no more, due to the imminent electrification and resignalling. The first photo shows the view from the country end of the station and includes Blackpool North No. 2 signal box. The second photo shows No. 47525 arriving with the 12.15 from Euston. 31 May 1991.

The first line to Morecambe was opened by the North Western Railway. The NWR was later absorbed by the Midland. The LNW opened its branch from Hest Bank to Morecambe in 1864. The MR line was electrified in 1908. Despite this it was closed in 1966 and it is the LNW line that survives.

A 'Pacer' departs from Morecambe with the 11.28 to Leeds. Note that two of the signal posts are wooden, and the other two concrete.

Morecambe signal box was a Midland Type 4b, constructed in 1907. It had a ninety-two-lever frame. It was abolished in 1994. Since these photographs were taken the original MR station has been closed and a new station built 400 metres to the east. The closure of the signal box has led to the simplification of the layout, with one line serving Morecambe station, and another serving Heysham. There is no connection between the two. 31 May 1990.

No. 143604 arrives at Oxenholme with the shuttle service from Windermere. Note the London Midland Region enamel sign. 31 May 1990.

No. 142037 arrives at Aspatria with a southbound service. The signal box has since been abolished.

No. 142037 once again, this time returning northbound at Wigton. The water column seems intact and ready for use!

On 10 August 1965 No. 44767 is seen at Wigton on a freight. This locomotive was constructed at Crewe in 1947 and fitted with Stephenson link motion. Happily, it has survived into preservation and is now named *George Stephenson*. (Photo: Peter Groom)

Near Grange over Sands, No. 60066 runs alongside the Kent estuary with a returning coal empties from Padiham power station. 6 June 1992.

Whitehaven. A Class 108 DMU arrives with the 09.10 Newcastle to Barrow. The box in the background is Bransty. The platform into which the train is running is now out of use and the line lifted. 2 June 1990.

These two photos perhaps illustrate as well as any, the dramatic changes that have taken place in the last thirty or forty years as regards freight traffic. The first photograph is taken from near Corkickle No. 1 box, looking towards Corkickle No. 2. The second photograph is taken from near No. 2 box, looking in the opposite direction. Everything in these photographs has now disappeared – track, sidings, gantry, signals, and both signal boxes. All that remains is a single track plain line. The train approaching Corkickle station is the 10.23 Barrow to Carlisle. 2 June 1990.

Settle and Carlisle

The line as far as Settle Junction was built by the NWR. The Midland wished to have an independent route to Scotland and obtained an Act in 1866 to build what later became known as the Settle and Carlisle line. Changed circumstances led to changed minds, and the Midland sought to abandon its plans. This they were denied by Parliament and construction went ahead, the line opening to goods traffic in November 1875 and to passengers in May 1876. The rundown of the line started after the Second World War, and was accelerated following the electrification of the WCML. Apart from Settle and Appleby, all other stations were closed in 1970.

By the 1980s it was clear that BR wished to close the line. In 1981 the Friends of the Settle–Carlisle Line was set up and started to fight a vigorous campaign against closure. As a result of this, passenger numbers rocketed, from 93,000 in 1983, to 450,000 in 1989, in which year the line was finally reprieved. Before this, in 1986, the area manager, Ron Cotton, had reopened some of the closed stations, and it was this that was partly responsible for the increase in passenger numbers.

Skipton on 11 June 1992. Points to note: the semaphore signals on wooden posts, one of which retains its finial; the parachute water column, and another on the adjacent platform; the beautiful glazed platform canopies; Skipton Station South signal box, just visible at the far right. The line in the right foreground is the Grassington branch. Much has subsequently changed here. Leeds to Skipton was electrified in 1994, leading to the removal of the signals and closure of the signal boxes. The line as far as Hellifield is now controlled from York.

A Class 144 unit departs from Skipton with the 13.03 Leeds to Lancaster. Skipton Station North signal box is in the background, also abolished. 11 June 1992.

In 1995, bearing the livery of one of the three short-lived freight companies into which Railfreight was divided in 1994, No. 60064 is seen on the Grassington branch with the Hull–Rylstone empties. The Grassington branch was all that was built of a line intended to reach the NER south of Darlington. Built by the Midland, it opened in 1902 and closed to passengers in 1930. It remains open for freight.

The railway reached Hellifield in 1849 with the opening of the North Western Railway's line from Skipton to Ingleton. It became a junction in 1880 when it was reached by the L&Y line from Blackburn.

On a dismal March day in 1989, No. 47569 arrives at Hellifield with the 10.45 Leeds to Carlisle.

On the same date Nos 20045 and 20159 approach the station from the north with a steel train diverted from the WCML. The Class 20 was the first main line diesel to be introduced under the 1955 Modernisation Plan, the first examples entering service in 1957. A total of 228 were built between 1957 and 1968. Of simple but robust construction, equipped with the English Electric 1,000hp 8SVT engine, they proved to be a very successful and long-lived design, a few remaining in service to this day (2017).

No. 47532 passes the redundant signal box at Horton-in-Ribblesdale with the diverted 10.25 Glasgow–Euston. 4 March 1989.

No. 47459 is seen pulling into Garsdale with the 15.16 Carlisle–Leeds. 22 September 1990.

The popularity of the line with hikers is evident as this Carlisle–Leeds service arrives at Kirkby Stephen. 11 March 1989.

No. 47488 *Rail Riders* stands at Appleby with the 12.42 Carlisle–Leeds. 11 March 1989.

Wennington, once the junction of lines to Carnforth and Lancaster, no longer even merits a signal box, which has been mostly switched out since 1988 and was abolished in 2006. The 12.33 Leeds to Morecambe departs from the deserted station. 31 May 1990.

North Cheshire and North Derbyshire

The Chester & Birkenhead Railway opened its line in September 1840, becoming part of the Birkenhead, Lancashire & Cheshire Junction Railway in 1847. The latter company opened the line from Chester to Warrington in December 1850. In August 1859, the BL&CJ was taken over by the GWR and LNWR to become the Birkenhead Joint – an identity it retained until nationalisation.

The Cheshire Midland Railway built the line from Atrincham to Northwich in 1863, while the West Cheshire Railway extended the line to Helsby in 1869. These two companies became part of the Cheshire Lines Committee, which was a joint railway owned by the GNR, MS&L and MR.

Nos 20154 and 20186 head through Helsby with a train bound for Fiddlers Ferry power station. The station master's house, the station buildings and the signal box are all listed structures. The signal box is a LNW Type 4 dating from 1900. The line to the left is to Chester, and that to the right to Stanlow and Hooton. 3 June 1991.

From the opposite direction No. 40107 approaches with a train of ballast. 2 September 1981.

The line to Hooton opened on 1 July 1863. This is Thornton South Sidings. Hard to believe perhaps, but everything here, apart from the main line over on the left, no longer exists. The signal box, also abolished, has found its way to the Embsay & Bolton Abbey Steam Railway. The photograph was taken on 29 April 1993 and shows Shell's No. 9 shunter at work.

Leasowe station opened and closed several times before remaining permanently open from 1894. It is a station on the electrified Merseyrail network. In this view taken on 17 February 1991, the train for West Kirby is being hand signalled over the crossing while new gates are installed. The signal box was abolished three years later.

No. 56093 passes Greenbank signal box with a train of MGR empties, which has just come from the ICI Winnington branch. Greenbank box is due to be abolished in 2017. 26 August 1994.

Near Delamere, No. 47368 heads east with a train of tanks. 2 September 1991.

No. 25249 at Northwich with a train of limestone bound for ICI Brunner Mond. 14 May 1981.

The CLC station at Helsby was called Helsby and Alvanley. The line, which branched off the Altrincham–Chester line at Mouldsworth, opened to freight on 1 September 1869 and to passengers the following May, but this service lasted only until 1875. It was reinstated for the summer months only between 1934 and 1938 and for workmen's trains between 1936 and 1944. Freight traffic ceased in the 1980s and the line was closed in 1992.

The LNWR built a line from Northwich to Sandbach in 1868 with a station at Middlewich, which lost its passenger service in 1959. The line remains open for freight and for diversions from the WCML as seen here. The 07.50 Euston–Holyhead passes through the site of Middlewich station. 10 May 1992.

Seen on 21 May 1991, No. 85110 has only a few months left in service before withdrawal later that year. One of a sub-class of fifteen locomotives modified for freight work, it is seen at Acton Bridge with a Dagenham–Halewood working.

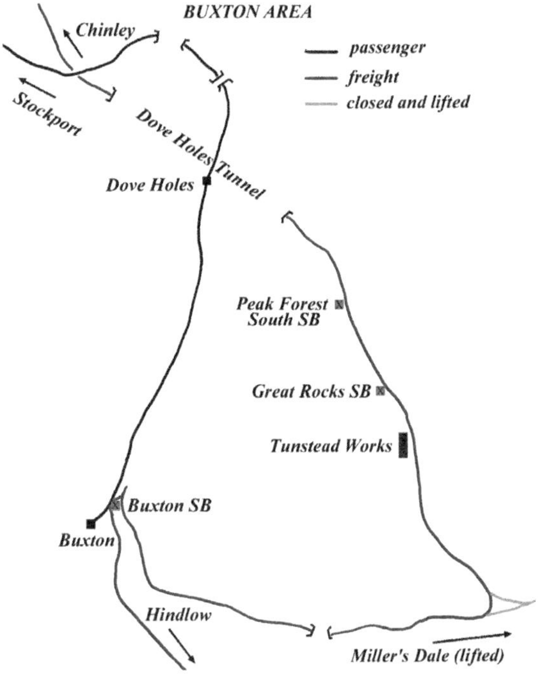

The Stockport, Disley & Whaley Bridge Railway completed its line to Buxton in 1863. In the same year the Midland Railway reached Buxton from the south. The SDWB was absorbed by the LNW in 1866. Meanwhile the Midland built a route as far as New Mills, from where it could access Manchester. This was completed in 1867. The LNW line from Ashbourne to Buxton via Hindlow was completed in 1894. The Ashbourne line lost its passenger service in 1954 and closed completely in 1967, except for the short section to Hindlow. The Midland route was closed to both passenger and freight between Matlock and Miller's Dale in 1968 but the line from Buxton to Manchester remained open for freight. The LNW route itself came close to closure in 1964. Buxton has for a long time been an important centre for the quarrying of limestone, all of which travels via the Midland line.

On 12 October 1981, No. 25106 climbs the 1 in 90 gradient at Peak Forest with a Tunstead–Northwich train. Banking assistance is being given by 25202.

At Peak Forest No. 25081 brings a train of limestone forward from the loading facility into the down sidings. The building on the right has since been demolished. Buxton Lime Firms is now part of Tarmac. 25 September 1981.

The British Railways Class 25 machines were doughty little engines. Although only equipped with the six-cylinder 1,250hp Sulzer engine, they were for many years entrusted with the heavy limestone trains which ran between Buxton and Northwich. After the last were withdrawn in 1987 a number of other types were used, including as seen here, Class 37s. This particular train, hauled by No. 37688, is a Tunstead to Hindlow working, seen between Buxton and Hindlow. 14 April 1993.

In 1994 the ICI wagons used on the Tunstead–Hindlow trains were replaced by the air-braked wagons seen here. The train also has new motive power, as No. 60089 approaches Buxton signal box with a train from Tunstead.

In May 1992, No. 150144 heads towards Buxton station with a service from Manchester. In 2017 there are twenty trains on weekdays between Manchester and Buxton, giving a basic hourly service. Journey time is about one hour. Some of these trains start back at Blackpool. In 1960 there were also twenty trains, also taking about an hour, so in fifty-seven years, zero progress!

Woodhead

Construction of the Woodhead Line was begun in 1841 by the Sheffield, Ashton-under-Lyne & Manchester Railway. Manchester–Woodhead was completed in 1844, and Sheffield–Dunford Bridge in July 1845. The 3-mile 22-yard Woodhead Tunnel was completed in December that year. A second bore was completed in 1852. In 1936 the LNER started work on electrifying the line at 1500 V dc. Work stopped at the outbreak of the Second World War. In 1948 a new tunnel was started and completed in 1954. Passenger services ceased in 1970 and the line was closed completely in July 1981.

Two types of locomotive were designed by the LNER to work the line, although all but one were actually built by BR. These were the 2,490hp Co-Co Class 77, and the 1,868hp Bo-Bo Class 76.

Penistone. Most trains on the Woodhead Route were double-headed, but in this instance we see a lone No. 76040 passing Huddersfield Junction signal box with a westbound train of coal in 14-ton mineral wagons, still a common sight in 1980.

More conventionally, Nos 76032 and 76033 pass with a train of LPG tanks.

Checking the catenary height. 27 May 1980.

At Dunford Bridge, Nos 76007 and 76012 hauling No. 45034 and a brake van emerge from the tunnel. The semaphore arm has lost its green spectacle glass.

Heading in the other direction are Nos 76006 and 76010 with more coal wagons. 18 April 1981.

Dunford Bridge in 1989.

An empty MGR train passes through the closed Woodhead station.

West Yorkshire/Diggle

A Class 40 stands at Leeds with a summer Saturdays Blackpool–Newcastle service on 4 July 1981. This was one of the few Trans-Pennine services worked by this class of locomotive at that time.

The majority of trains were handled by Class 45, 46 or 47 machines, as in this photo, which shows No. 47405 hauling the 11.17 Newcastle–Liverpool, seen near Marsden on 17 April in the same year.

An unidentified Class 46 passes Diggle Junction signal box with the 10.05 Liverpool–Newcastle. 17 April 1981.

Ten years later, No. 47704 is seen at the same location with the 10.20 Newcastle–Liverpool. This was the penultimate day of loco-haulage on this route. Note that the 47 is in Scotrail livery. 19 January 1991.

Above and below: The construction of the Trans-Pennine route via Diggle had a protracted and complicated history. Initially promoted by the Huddersfield & Manchester Railway & Canal Company (H&M) and the Leeds, Dewsbury & Manchester Railway Company, by the time it was completed in 1849 both were part of the LNW. Huddersfield station itself was a joint enterprise of the LNW and L&Y. According to John Betjeman, Huddersfield station had the 'most splendid station façade in England'. Unsurprisingly, it is a listed building. Also listed is the goods warehouse, together with the hydraulic lift, which was used to take wagons up to the second floor. On a siding two ex-LMS brake wagons await their fate. 21 August 1989.

The route via Diggle was not the first railway through the Pennines. The route via the Calder Valley opened in 1841. The section of this route between Milner Royd Junction and Bradley Junction lost its passenger service in 1970 but regained it in 2000 with the opening of Brighouse station. Just west of Brighouse No. 37717 heads east with a tank train. 25 July 1994.

Further east along this line is Healey Mills Yard. Extending over 140 acres, the yard opened in 1963 and was designed to be able to process 4,000 wagons per day. It closed as a marshalling yard in 1987 but was retained for stabling locomotives and rolling stock until its definitive closure in 2012. No. 60066, in the livery of the ephemeral Transrail company, passes through the yard with a Bredbury–Roxby 'binliner'.

The Huddersfield & Sheffield Junction Railway opened its line from Huddersfield to Penistone in 1850. At Penistone it joined the Manchester, Sheffield & Lincolnshire Railway. On 27 May 1980, a Class 101 unit approaches Penistone station with the 16.22 Huddersfield–Sheffield. The 330-yard-long Penistone Viaduct has been the scene of a number of accidents, most spectacularly on 2 February 1916 when the viaduct collapsed under L&Y 2-4-2T No. 661. The crew were able to jump clear but the tank was not so lucky and was cut up on site.

Castleford was at the end of the long reach of the NER, as the NER Type S1a signal box attests. The box was opened in 1882 and closed in 1997, and the magnificent array of signals are no more. A new signal box, 'Castleton', has been built in the V of the Pontefract lines (to the left) and the Normanton lines (straight on). The Leeds–Knottingley/Nottingham trains all reverse here. The line to Milford Junction is freight only. On 27 August 1989, No. 150240 arrives with a Sheffield–Leeds service.

Just north of Royston, No. 56074 passes south with a train of MGR empties, probably heading for Grimethorpe colliery. Note that at the date of this photograph, 18 April 81, this was still a four-track railway. In fact until 1968 this was the main route between Sheffield and Leeds. Between the wars this line saw the passage of the Bradford–St Pancras 'Yorkshireman'. In 1968, due to subsidence, passenger traffic was switched to the Swinton & Knottingley line but reverted to this line in 1972. In the early 1980s it switched back once more to the Swinton & Knottingley line and in 1988 the line was closed to through traffic.

By 1994 it had become a double-track railway. No. 58012 heads north with a train of empties ex-Grimethorpe Coalite. It was on this day – 31 March 1994 – that the closure of the Coalite plant was announced.

Also on 31 March, No. 58026 is seen at the site of Royston and Notton station heading south with a train of sand for Monk Bretton. This is the only traffic now seen on this line, which has been reduced to just a single track.

At a similar location, No. 44538 heads a long mineral train southwards in July 1951. (Photo: Ben Brooksbank)

The Leeds & Bradford Railway built the line through Bingley and Shipley to Skipton, opening in 1847. The line was leased by the Midland in 1846, then purchased in 1851.

A Skipton–Leeds train approaches Shipley station. From the triangular station at Shipley, lines radiate out to Bradford, Leeds, Ilkley and Skipton. This scene has changed dramatically. At the time this photograph was taken there were three signal boxes at Shipley, as well as others on the radiating lines. All have now gone and the lines have been electrified. Signalling is controlled from York. 21 August 1989.

South Yorkshire

Sheffield had to wait until 1870 before it had a direct route south to London. George Stephenson's aversion to anything but minimal gradients led the North Midland Railway to bypass Sheffield, which was then served by a branch from Rotherham. The Sheffield & Rotherham Railway opened its line in 1838 and was absorbed by the Midland in 1845.

Old railway; a pair of Class 31s take on water in order to supply steam heat to Mark 1 carriages. This is the 08.35 Taunton to Newcastle headed by Nos 31260 and 31209, seen at Sheffield on 29 October 1981.

No. 46036 stands at Sheffield with the 07.17 Harwich Parkeston Quay to Manchester Piccadilly. Known universally as 'The Boat Train', it was a regular turn for a Class 46. 10 February 1982.

A Class 110 DMU stands at Sheffield waiting for its next duty. Known as 'Calder Valley' units, they were a development of Class 104, also built by the Birmingham Railway Carriage & Wagon Company. They were fitted with 180hp Rolls-Royce engines, better enabling them to tackle the hilly countryside in South and West Yorkshire. Introduced in 1962, the last were withdrawn in 1990. 29 October 1981.

On the same day, also at Sheffield, is prototype 'Pacer' No. 140001. Introduced in 1980, it was only ever used for testing and crew training. It was equipped with 200hp Leyland engines and automatic transmission. It has survived into preservation and is now at the Keith & Dufftown Railway.

Jubilee No. 45730 *Ocean* stands at Sheffield, having arrived with a train from Bristol. An early member of the class was named *Silver Jubilee* in honour of the silver jubilee of King George V. The name then came to be applied to the whole class. Designed under the direction of William Stanier, there was a total of 191 Jubilees. Classified 5XP by the LMS, they later became 6P5F under BR. They were the mainstay of express services on the Midland main line. (Photo: Ben Brooksbank, 18 March 1961)

Work on Tinsley Marshalling Yard started in August 1961, with commissioning taking place in October 1965. There were eleven reception sidings, fifty-three main sorting sidings, and twenty-five secondary sorting sidings. The yard was designed to have a capacity of handling 275 trains per 24 hours. Tinsley started to be run down from 1984. When this photograph was taken in August 1992, the yard was still relatively complete, although clearly massively underused. The connections at the eastern end of the yard (the end from which this photograph was taken) were severed in 1993. Tinsley Traction Maintenance Depot closed in 1998. Today, no more than seven or eight sidings remain in use for the Sheffield International Freight Terminal.

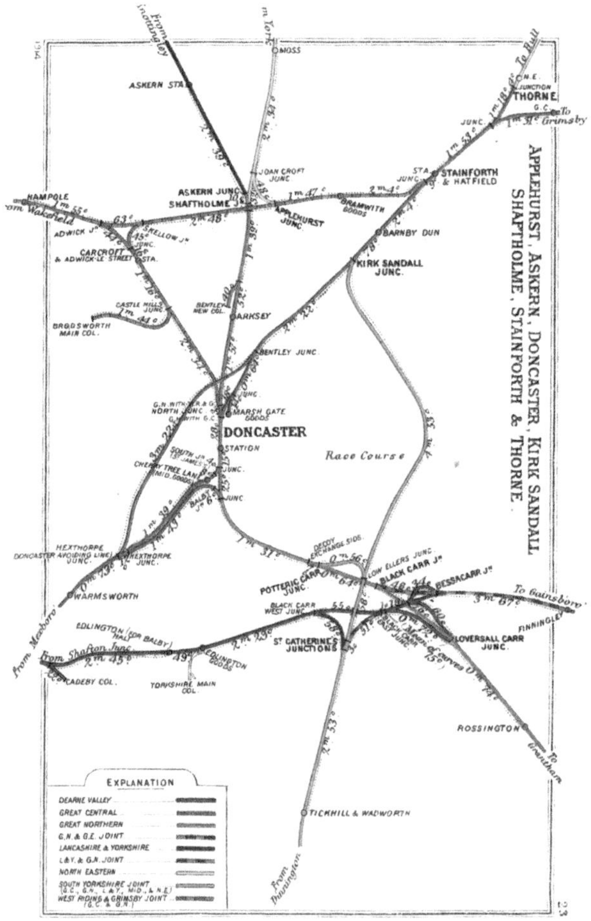

Left: The complicated set-up around Doncaster.

Below: No. 37512 heads east with a train of tanks on the Adwick–Stainforth freight-only line.

No. 158766 heads east through Kirk Sandall Junction. 1993.

On 27 February 1993 No. 56102 with an MGR train passes Ferrybridge signal box. In the background is the vast bulk of Ferrybridge B power station, closed the previous year and subsequently demolished. The signal box has been closed and replaced by a new signalling centre on the other side of the tracks, also named Ferrybridge.

Drax power station, with its 3,960 megawatt capacity, consumed up to 36,000 tonnes of coal per day. On 5 September 1992, No. 56095 leaves with empties as in the background another train arrives to discharge its load. The Yorkshire coalfields are now part of history.

Selby

The station at Selby came into being with the opening of the Leeds & Selby Railway in September 1834. Connection with York was achieved in 1839 when the York & North Midland completed the line from York to Milford, on the Leeds & Selby. In 1871, the NER opened a line from Shaftholme Junction via Selby to York. This formed part of what later became the East Coast Main Line. In 1983, in order that the new Selby coalfield could be exploited, a diversion of the ECML was built from Templehirst Junction to Colton Junction, thus avoiding Selby. The opening of the new line saw the simultaneous closure of the line north from Selby to York. On 10 September 1981, No. 55021 calls at Selby with the 12.05 King's Cross to York. Selby has listed building status, this listing including the canopies, parts of which can be seen in this view. The central through lines at Selby have been removed.

South of Selby is Brayton Junction. This is where a spur from the main line diverged to meet the NER line from Thorpe Gates to Goole. This line was opened in 1910 and closed in 1964. No. 55008 heads past with the 10.47 York to King's Cross, 10 September 1981. At this point the Deltics had just a few months left in service, as the remaining examples were withdrawn from normal service at the end of the year. Equipped with two high-speed diesel engines, originally developed for marine use, the Deltics were for a long time the most powerful diesel locomotives on British Railways. There were just twenty-two machines in the class, of which six survived into preservation. Brayton Junction signal box has been abolished.

East Riding

The Hull & Selby Railway opened their line in 1840. The line to the left is to Goole and Doncaster, opened by the NER in 1869. Until 1975 Gilberdyke Junction and the adjacent station went under the name of Staddlethorpe. On 31 March 1990, No. 156467 heads towards Hull with a service from Manchester Piccadilly.

This photograph, taken on 5 September 1992, shows the yard at Goole full of disused wagons. This tranquil scene is no more as the sidings have now all been removed.

The Hull & Selby Railway built the line from Hull to Bridlington, while the York & North Midland constructed the section from Seamer to Bridlington. Both sections opened on 6 October 1846. The station at Beverley, as well as others along this section of line, was designed by G. T. Andrews. A Class 101 DMU has arrived with a service for Hull. Beverley is a listed building.

Nafferton. A Class 101 DMU departs with the 16.27 Scarborough to Hull. 10 August 1989. The signal box was abolished shortly after this photograph was taken and the crossing converted to automatic half barriers. The NER box dates from 1906 and has listed status. Despite this, it has been demolished.

Quay Crossing is just north of Bridlington. The driver of the 14.05 Hull to Scarborough is collecting the token for the single line section to Hunmanby. The signal box was closed in 1998 and subsequently demolished. 30 December 1990.

Left and below: Bridlington, another listed structure, dating from 1912, when the station was rebuilt. The rebuild included the construction of the magnificent glass and cast-iron canopies above platforms 5 and 6. The canopy at the front of the station dates from the original G. T. Andrews building of 1846. Note that the 'Refreshments' sign is in North Eastern Region orange. 10 August 1989.

At Hunmanby a Class 101 DMU waits to depart with a service to Bridlington on 10 August 1989. The crossing gates have now been replaced by automatic barriers and the signal box closed.

North Yorkshire

The first temporary station at York was constructed in 1839, ready for the arrival of the York & North Midland Railway line from Milford. The following year, with the construction of the link to Altofts Junction, a through route to London was completed. This ran via the North Midland as far as Derby, and then via the Midland Counties and the London & Birmingham. The present station dates from 1877 and is a listed building.

Scarborough station was designed by G. T. Andrews and opened in 1845 with the completion of the York & North Midland's line from York. The station was at its busiest in the inter-war years. On August bank holiday 1939, 102 arrivals and 106 departures were scheduled. Somewhat reduced in size from those days, Scarborough today has just five platforms. This view was taken from the country end of platform 1 in September 1989.

The wonderful array of semaphore signals at Falsgrave. Despite its name, the signal box is actually situated at the end of platform one of Scarborough station. The box, which is an NER Southern Division Type 4, dates from 1908 and contains a 120-lever frame. Sadly no longer in use, it is a listed structure. The gantry, constructed by McKenzie & Holland in 1911 is also listed. It now resides at Grosmont on the North York Moors Railway. The second photograph, taken slightly further back, shows a bracket signal with wooden dolls. To the left of the signal box can be seen the tunnel that formerly led to the Whitby line, closed in 1965. Trains from Scarborough had to be hauled out of the station beyond the tunnel; the engine then ran round the train before heading off to Whitby. In the main picture, No. 156489 passes under the gantry with the 14.20 Scarborough to Liverpool. 24 September 1989.

Seamer West Junction. The lines to the left are to York, those to the right are to Bridlington and Hull. The signal box also controlled the line to Pickering, which closed in 1950. The box, which dates from 1908, was abolished in 2000. The junction is now controlled by Seamer signal box. 24 September 1989.

Seamer, and yes, there are two signal boxes. The one on the right is the original York & North Midland Railway box, which closed in 1911 when the new one came into use. This was known as Seamer East, until Seamer West was abolished, and has since been renamed Seamer. Since this photograph was taken the old signal box has been demolished, as has the platform canopy, which has been replaced by a bus shelter-type structure. The station building is on the far left. 10 August 1989.

Weaverthorpe signal box remains in use, unlike its station, which closed along with all but one of the other sixteen stations along the York–Scarborough line back in 1930. The sole survivor is Malton. The reason for this wholesale closure was the need not to impede the intensive excursion traffic heading for Scarborough. A Class 156 passes with a service for Scarborough. 24 August 1989.

No shortage of steam for No. 40015 as it awaits a crew change at York while in charge of the 08.05 Liverpool to Newcastle. 16 December 1981.

Passing Holgate junction as it pulls away from York is No. 45137 *Bedfordshire and Hertfordshire Regiment (TA)* with the 09.05 Edinburgh–Plymouth on 31 August 1981. The six tracks seen here were subsequently reduced to four and electrification reached York in 1989, the same year that the last of the 'Peaks' was withdrawn.

The line from York to Knaresborough, where it made connection with the Leeds & Thirsk Railway, was constructed in 1848 by the East & West Yorkshire Junction Railway, later absorbed by the York & North Midland. Originally double track, sections of the line, including here at Marston Moor, were singled in 1973. Discussions are under way with a view to reinstating double track and electrifying the line. Marston Moor station was closed in 1958. The gate box, which is a listed building, remains open. The lever frame inside is thought to date from 1873. On 13 October 1990, a York–Leeds 'Pacer' passes over the level crossing.

The line from Northallerton to Leyburn was constructed by the York, Newcastle & Berwick Railway between 1848 and 1858. Leyburn to Hawes was built by the NER, and Garsdale to Hawes by the Midland Railway. The NER section lost its passenger service in 1954, the Midland section provided a passenger service until 1959. Freight continued, in later years to serve only the quarry at Redmire. Subsequently the MOD took an interest in the line, in order to transport tanks to its Catterick base. In 2000 the Wensleydale Railway plc took out a lease on the line and from 2003 has run passenger services. A number of stations have been reopened.

Bedale signal box and crossing.

The Bedale signalman and the crew of No. 60031, with the empties for Redmire, exchange tokens. 29 May 1992.

As the returning loaded train approaches the level crossing at Wensley station a member of the crew descends to open the crossing gates.

The train having passed, the third member of the crew, travelling in the guard's van, closes the gates. This traffic ceased shortly after these photographs were taken. 29 May 1992.

Above left: The North Yorkshire & Cleveland Railway opened the line from Picton to Grosmont, on the Malton–Whitby line, in 1858. Battersby Junction came into being with the opening of the Ingleby–Nunthorpe line in 1868. It was originally known as Ingleby Junction. A freight line from Battersby to Rosedale was constructed in 1861, thus making Battersby a four-way junction. Picton–Battersby lost its passenger service in 1954, with freight following later. Subsequently, trains to Grosmont and Whitby were routed via Middlesbrough, which entailed a reversal at Battersby. A Class 143 'Pacer' arrives at Battersby with a Whitby–Middlesbrough service. This scene has changed considerably; the signal box and semaphore signals have all gone and there is now only one platform line. The junction is controlled from Nunthorpe.

Above right: The Stockton & Darlington Railway extended its line to Middlesbrough in 1830. Before the railway arrived, the settlement had a population of just forty. It was the arrival of the railway and the subsequent industrial development that made the town what it is. No. 56085 is seen heading away from Middlesbrough with a train of coke. The lines in the centre of the photo, behind the train, lead to Middlesbrough Goods Depot.

Having deposited his train in ICI's Haverton Hill Sidings (seen on the right), the driver of No. 56034 surrenders the token for the single line before heading away light engine. The line straight on leads to Seal Sands. 05 April 1994.

The North East

The line along the Durham coast took sixty-five years to complete and involved six different companies. First on the scene was the Stockton & Hartlepool Railway, which opened its line in 1841. Lord Londonderry built a line from Seaham to Hendon via Ryhope to enable the export of coal from his mines. This was not converted for passenger use until 1900, after which it was worked by the NER. The final piece in the jigsaw was put in place by the NER when it completed the line between Hartlepool and Seaham.

A Class 143 'Pacer' passes Clarence Road signal box as it approaches Hartlepool station with the 11.45 Hexham–Middlesbrough on 4 May 1991. Clarence Road box was taken out of use in 2010 and demolished the same year.

A Class 143 DMU arrives at Seaham with the 14.03 Middlesbrough to Newcastle. The subsidiary signal, now removed, would have controlled the line to Seaham Docks. Following the Durham coast resignalling, Seaham was retained to control the pedestrian crossing. When this was replaced by an underpass in 2013 the box was finally closed. This line is now controlled from Ryhope Grange.

Lord Londonderry had a private station at Hall Dene. He had the right to stop any train, with the exception of expresses. This arrangement continued until 1924. The station is seen in its later years. The station building still stands.

The line from Ryhope to Sunderland Docks has only ever been a freight line. On 5 April 1994, the driver climbs aboard No. 60028 preparing to leave Hendon with a train of tanks. This line closed the following year but was reopened in February 2015.

The Newcastle & Carlisle Railway opened its line in stages, from March 1835 to June 1838. The company remained independent until its absorption by the NER in 1862. The line retains many original features, a large number of which are listed structures. Included among them is the gantry signal box at Hexham, which dates from 1897. 'Pacer' No. 143613 approaches the station with a service for Carlisle. 29 August 1991.

A view from the signal box as a pair of Class 108 units head towards Carlisle. Little has changed at Hexham since this photograph was taken on 19 February 1990. The station buildings and canopies at Hexham also have listed status.

No. 156463 arrives at Haltwhistle with a Carlisle service. The branch to Alton opened in 1852. It crossed the South Tyne by the viaduct that can be seen on the right. It closed as late as 1976. 29 August 1991.

This train is from the Melkridge opencast site. At the time the photograph was taken the signalling at Melkridge had not been fully installed so that trains had to leave westbound to Carlisle, as this train is doing, before running round and heading back east. Denton Village Crossing box remains in use. Notice the unusual signal post.

Brampton Fell signal box is another which remains in use. At Brampton there was once a branch to Brampton Town. This closed back in 1923. A Class 156 passes with an eastbound service. 28 August 1991.

No. 40130 stands at Newcastle having arrived with the 08.53 from Blackpool. 4 July 1981.

No. 37250 heads south through Bedlington with a train of steel ingots. This locomotive has survived into preservation and is to be found on the Wensleydale Railway.

Winning signal box and the view towards North Blyth. Winning sits at the junction of the lines to Ashington and Bedlington. The main signal on the bracket is for Bedlington, while the subsidiary is for Ashington. 05 May 1991.

The West Highland Line

The railway at Oban was constructed by the Callander & Oban Railway. Callander had been reached by the Dunblane, Doune & Callander Railway (DDC) in 1858. It was then proposed to build a railway from Callander, via Crainlarich to Oban. The DDC was absorbed by the Scottish Central Railway on 31 July 1865, which in turn was taken over by the Caledonian Railway the following day. The line reached Tyndrum in 1873, Dalmally in 1877, and Oban in June 1880. The connection at Crianlarich into the North British Fort William line was not made until 1897. Dunblane to Crianlarich closed in September 1965.

The Place family, who owned the land at Crianlarich, were not at all happy at the arrival of the railway, fearing that it would spoil their shooting grounds, and refused to sell the required land, which in the end had to be compulsorily purchased. Shortly after, they sold up and went off in a huff to Yorkshire.

The Class 27 had a strong association with the West Highland Line. These locomotives were built by the Birmingham Railway Carriage & Wagon Company in 1961/62 and powered by the Sulzer 6LDA28B engine, an up-rated version of the engine fitted to the Class 26. They were initially allocated to various regions, before eventually all making their way to Scotland. They differed from the Class 26 in having a headcode box and a top speed of 90 mph compared to the Class 26's 80 mph.

On 19 June 1980, Nos 27042 and 27002 stand at Oban waiting to leave with the 17.48 to Glasgow. The semaphore signals were removed in 1982, following the introduction of electronic token working.

This is the original Oban station, also seen in June 1980. Despite being a listed building it was demolished in 1986 and replaced with a smaller structure.

At Crianlarich the signalman chats with the driver of a southbound mixed freight headed by No. 27110. There is no longer a signalman here. Radio Electronic Tokenless Block, controlled from Banavie, was introduced for the whole of the West Highland Line in 1987.

Coal merchants shovel coal from a BR 14-ton mineral wagon. Note that Crianlarich retains the name 'Upper' despite being renamed simply 'Crianlarich' in 1965 after the closure of Crianlarich Lower.

Above: A Class 27 crosses the River Fillan as it approaches Crianlarich with the 07.00 Mallaig to Glasgow. 17 June 1980.

Right: Having made its call at Crianlarich, the engine makes a brisk start away from the station with its rake of Mark 1 coaches.

At Garelochhead No. 27002 arrives with the 12.53 Glasgow–Oban to pick up a lone passenger. Notice the island platform and chalet-style station building, typical of this line. 19 June 80.

The 07.00 Mallaig–Glasgow arrives at Rannoch Station. The carving is of John Renton, a man who gave part of his fortune in order that the West Highland would be completed. There can be few more lonely and isolated stations than Rannoch, sitting as it does in the middle of nowhere, remote from any settlement. 19 June 1990.

Stirling to Aberdeen

On 24 March 1991, the Inverness–Kings Cross 'Highland Chieftain' arrives at Stirling. On the left is Stirling North box. The pair of lines on the right leads to the Stirling and Dunfermline line. After this line lost its passenger service in 1968, sections of track at each end of the line were kept in place for freight services. However, the middle section, which included Alloa, was lifted. In 2008 the passenger service to a new station at Alloa was reinstated and the inhabitants of that town now enjoy an hourly service to/from Glasgow.

The line from Greenhill Junction, on the Edinburgh & Glasgow Railway, to Perth was opened by the Scottish Central Railway in 1848. The present Stirling station was built in 1915 and is a Grade A listed structure. Also listed Grade A are Stirling North signal box – a Caledonian Railway Type 2, with a forty-eight-lever frame – Stirling Middle signal box – also a Caledonian Railway Type 2, with a ninety-six-lever frame – and the semaphore signals in the station area. A pair of Class 158s arrive with the 11.25 Glasgow Queen St. to Aberdeen.

The present day line from Perth to Inverness was built by five different companies. Between Perth and Dundee it was the work of the Dundee & Perth Railway, later part of the Caledonian. At Errol, No. 158706 passes with a southbound service. The signal box is a Caledonian Type 1, dating from 1877. It is one of the oldest signal boxes in Scotland and is a listed structure. The station, closed since 1985, is also listed.

The spectacularly unusual station of Brought Ferry. The Dundee & Arbroath Railway was constructed in 1838 to a gauge of 5 feet 6 inches. In 1848 it was converted to standard gauge, the same year that a branch to the ferry pier was opened. In 1863 it became part of the Scottish North Eastern Railway, and then the Caledonian. In 1880 the railway became a joint line with the North British. The station and signal box are both listed Grade A; it is the oldest working station in Scotland. Sadly, the unique footbridge, which passed through the base of the signal box, has been removed and the redundant signal box relocated. A southbound HST approaches the station. 25 March 1991.

The North British opened the Arbroath & Montrose Railway in 1881 for goods and in 1883 for passengers. The line was partly doubled in 1897; the remainder between 1928 and 1932. Inverkeilor lost its station as early as 1930. The signal box dates from 1881 and is one of the few NBR boxes remaining operational. The 12.28 Aberdeen–Glasgow passes the box.

The Aberdeen Railway built the line from Guthrie to Aberdeen, which opened in stages between February 1848 and April 1850. Several mergers later, the line became part of the Caledonian. Only the section between Kinnaber Junction and Aberdeen survives. Laurencekirk station closed in 1967, but a vigorous local campaign saw it reopen in 2009 and the station has been completely restored. Passenger numbers have far exceeded expectations. No. 158732 passes the still closed station with the 14.28 Aberdeen–Glasgow. 25 March 1991.

Aberdeen to Inverness

The Great North of Scotland Railway was formed in 1845 to build a line from Aberdeen to Inverness. By 1854 it had completed the line from Kittybrewster to Huntly; by 1856 the extension from Kittybrewster to Aberdeen, and by 1858 the 12.5 miles from Huntly to Keith. The station at Dyce opened in 1854, closed in 1968, and reopened in 1984. The signal box dates from 1880. In 2007 the semaphores were replaced by colour lights. In 2009 the Raiths Farm freight terminal was opened adjacent to the station. No. 47323 waits to enter the single line section to Aberdeen with a Speedlink service. The Class 156 arriving is the 09.14 Aberdeen to Thurso.

No. 47526 waits in the loop at Inverurie with another southbound Speedlink train. At its peak, the Speedlink service was carrying 8 million tonnes per annum. It closed down not long after these photographs were taken. 26 March 1991.

The splendid wooden station of Kennethmont, closed in 1968.

No. 156496 passes Kennethmont signal box with the 09.57 Thurso to Aberdeen. The box was constructed by the Railway Signal Company in 1880.

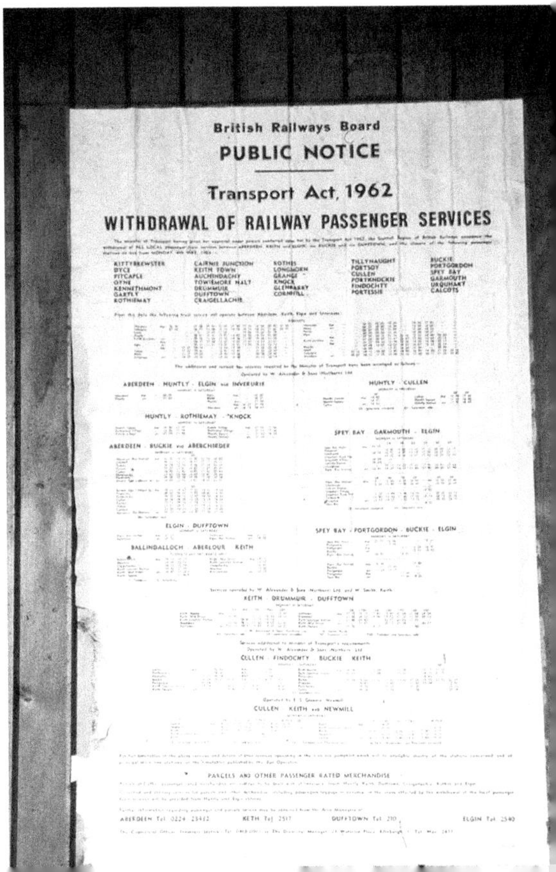

The original closure notice, posted inside the station, and still in good condition in 1991. 26 March 1991.

Keith Town (GNOS) looking north towards Keith (HR). The Keith & Dufftown Railway opened in 1862 and was worked by the GNOS, which extended the line to Boat of Garten in 1866. This section lost its passenger service in 1965, and Keith Town to Dufftown in 1968. This latter section was retained for freight and was still active when this photograph was taken in 1991. A preservation group took over the line in 1998 and have been running trains since 2000. They own a number of diesel multiple units and industrial shunters.

At Forres, the signalman and driver of an Inverness–Aberdeen service prepare to exchange tokens. Forres became a junction in 1863 when the Inverness & Perth Junction Railway opened its line to Boat of Garten. 26 March 1991.

It was the constituent companies of the Highland Railway who completed the line to Inverness. The Inverness & Nairn Railway opened in November 1855, and in August 1858 the Inverness & Aberdeen Junction Railway opened the Nairn–Keith line, thus completing the route all the way from Inverness to the south. These two companies merged in 1861.

The Far North Line

Promoted by the Inverness & Ross-shire Railway, the line from Inverness to Thurso and Wick opened in stages between 1862 and 1874. Dingwall was reached in 1862, Invergordon in 1863, Helmsdale in 1871 – after which the line was worked by the HR – and finally Wick and Thurso in July 1874.

At Inverness No. 26039 waits to leave with the 11.10 to Thurso and Wick on 13 June 1980.

Between 1958 and 1959, the Birmingham Railway Carriage & Wagon Company supplied BR with twenty Bo-Bo locomotives powered by the 1,160hp Sulzer 6LA28 engine. These machines, later designated 26/0, were supplied to the Eastern Region. BRCW supplied a further twenty-seven locomotives of a slightly modified design (26/1), which went directly to the Scottish Region in 1959. In 1960 the 26/0 class was also allocated to the Scottish Region. These robust little engines became the Scottish Region maid-of-all-work and were found on a variety of duties. They were particularly associated with the Far North Line and the Highland Main Line. From the early 1980s they started to be replaced on passenger duties by classes 37 and 47 but continued on other work until the last was withdrawn in 1993, thus lasting longer in service than the more powerful Class 27. Thirteen of the class have survived into preservation.

No. 26039 runs round the same train at Helmsdale. The train had to be terminated here due to a freight derailment further north.

The Highland Main Line

In 1856, the Perth & Dunkeld Railway opened its line between Stanley Junction and Dunkeld. The Inverness & Perth Junction Railway constructed the line from Forres to Dunkeld, which was fully open by September 1863. In 1865 the Inverness & Aberdeen Junction and the Inverness & Perth Junction railways merged to form the Highland Railway. In order to shorten the route between Inverness and Perth, the HR later built the line from Aviemore to Inverness, completing this in 1898. The original Forres–Aviemore line closed in 1965.

At Blair Atholl on 27 March 1991 'The Clansman' (11.10 Inverness–Euston) waits for the late-running 09.55 Glasgow–Inverness to clear the section before continuing with its journey.

On the same day, No. 158704 passes through Kingussie with a service for Glasgow. The signal box is a McKenzie & Holland Type 3 of 1894. Both it and the station buildings are Grade B listed structures.

Glasgow and South Western

Nos 37801 and 37170 blast up the gradient on their way to Killoch Washery.

At Waterside Nos 37505 and 37069 are seen with a train of coal, ex-Chalmerston opencast. 1 August 1995.

A pair of Class 318 units pass through the yard at Ayr with the 07.58 Ayr–Glasgow. 1 August 1995.

These three photographs were taken at Barrhill, which is an intermediate stop on the Ayr–Stranraer line. The railway arrived here in 1877.

Above: This photograph shows a pair of Tyer's Electric Tablet No. 6 machines. These control the single lines south to Dunragit and north to Glenwhilly. This is the last place in Britain where Tyer's tablets are still used. The machines are located in the station office.

Left: The frame is located on the opposite platform in the G&SW cabin retrieved from Portpatrick.

Having obtained the token for the section to Dunragit, the crew of the track machine are about to depart for Stranraer. 28 March 1991.

At Dunragit, the signalman swaps tokens with the driver of a service heading for Stranraer. Dunragit signal box was built by the LMS in *c*. 1924 and is a listed building. Dunragit station closed in 1965.

No. 47453, bearing the name *Eland*, waits for its next duty at Stranraer.

Also at Stranraer, shunting is taking place in readiness for the afternoon's Speedlink departure. 28 March 1991.

At Eastriggs MOD, on the Gretna–Dumfries line, having arrived with the train on the left, No. 47293 waits to depart with the return working. 29 March 1991.

No. 47293, back on the main line, heads off south. The line here was singled in the early 1970s, and since this photograph was taken has once more been doubled.